Wow, That's Woolly!

LLAMAS

Gareth Stevens Publishing

Beth Gottlieb

Please visit our website, www.garethstevens.com. For a free color catalog of all our high-quality books, call toll free 1-800-542-2595 or fax 1-877-542-2596.

Library of Congress Cataloging-in-Publication Data
Names: Gottlieb, Beth, author.
Title: Llamas / Beth Gottlieb.
Description: New York : Gareth Stevens Publishing, [2023] | Series: Wow, that's woolly! | Includes index.
Identifiers: LCCN 2021058305 (print) | LCCN 2021058306 (ebook) | ISBN 9781538279489 (set) | ISBN 9781538279496 (library binding) | ISBN 9781538279472 (paperback) | ISBN 9781538279502 (ebook)
Subjects: LCSH: Llamas--Juvenile literature. | Wool--Juvenile literature.
Classification: LCC SF401.L6 G68 2023 (print) | LCC SF401.L6 (ebook) | DDC 636.2/966--dc23/eng/20211208
LC record available at https://lccn.loc.gov/2021058305
LC ebook record available at https://lccn.loc.gov/2021058306

Published in 2023 by
Gareth Stevens Publishing
29 E. 21st Street
New York, NY 10010

Designer: Olivia Lo Sardo
Editor: Kristen Nelson

Portions of this work were originally authored by Lori MacDhui and published as *Llamas*. All new material this edition authored by Beth Gottlieb.

Photo credits: Cover a_v_d/Shutterstock.com; llama silhouettes Maria Plakhotya; Map GoodStock/Shutterstock.com; p. 5 Jolanda Aalbers/Shutterstock.com; p. 6 Paulaparaula/Shutterstock.com; p. 7 Noe Besso/Shutterstock.com; p. 9 Inga Locmele/Shutterstock.com; p. 11 Jeff McCollough/Shutterstock.com; p. 13 Evgeny Subbotsky/Shutterstock.com; p. 15 LisaStelzel/Shutterstock.com; p. 17 SvetlanaSatsiuk/Shutterstock.com; p. 19 aroastockart/Shutterstock.com; p. 21 Suzanne Tucker/Shutterstock.com

Printed in the United States of America

CPSIA compliance information: Batch #CSGS23: For further information, contact Gareth Stevens, New York, New York, at 1-800-542-2595.

Find us on

CONTENTS

Words in the glossary appear in **bold** type the first time they are used in the text.

COOL LLAMAS

Llamas have become popular animals! Pictures of them are found on shirts, posters, and pillows. But there's more to these animals than just their cool **image**.

Llamas are part of the Camelidae family. They are related to camels, but they are more closely related to alpacas, guanacos, and vicuñas. Like camels and alpacas, llamas have a lovely wool people use to make cloth. Wool is the natural **fiber** that grows on some animals that's used to make goods.

PULL BACK THE WOOL

Llamas and alpacas are often confused for one another. In fact, llamas are almost twice as big as alpacas!

Do you think llamas are cute or funny looking?

LLAMA LOOKS

Llamas have long legs and a long neck. Adult llamas can stand almost 6 feet (1.8 m) tall at their head. They weigh between 250 and 450 pounds (113 and 204 kg). Llamas have small heads and large ears. Their teeth seem to stick out.

Llamas have special **adaptations** that help them in their mountain homes. Their feet have two toes and wide pads on the bottom for walking on rocky land. Llamas have thick coats to keep them warm in the windy mountains.

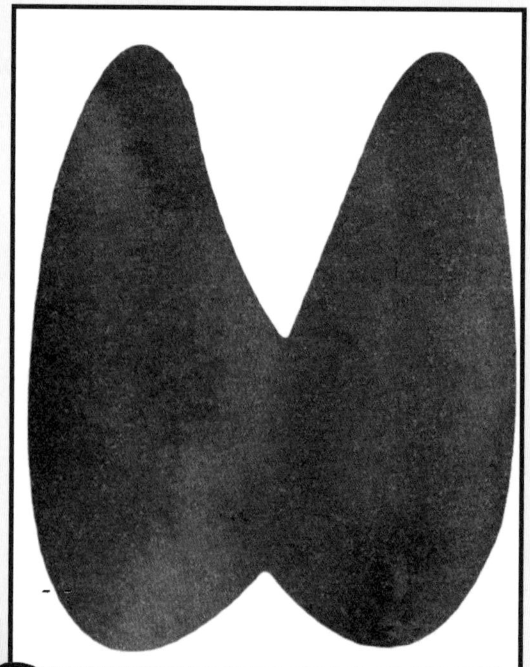

llama footprint

Many llamas are white, but they may also be gray, brown, red, or black.

LLAMA LIFE

Llamas are herbivores. That means they eat only plants. They're able to eat many different kinds of plants and don't need very much water.

Llamas like to live in groups called herds. They **communicate** with each other through sounds and by moving their ears and tails. Llamas hum when they're worried or uncomfortable. They cluck when they're meeting a new llama. When they sense danger, llamas will let out a high-pitched cry. This warns the rest of the herd to run away.

PULL BACK THE WOOL

Llamas can live for up to 20 years.

Today, all known llamas are **domesticated**. There are no wild herds.

MOTHERS AND BABIES

After llamas **mate**, female llamas carry a baby for about 11 months. They usually have one baby at a time. A baby llama is called a cria. Crias weigh between 18 and 33 pounds (8 and 15 kg) when they are born!

Baby llamas can stand soon after birth. Since llamas are **mammals**, babies drink milk made by their mother. When female llamas are about one year old, they can have babies of their own. Llamas often live between 15 and 20 years.

Baby llamas stay with their mother for many months.

IN HISTORY

Thousands of years ago, people living in the Andes Mountains domesticated llamas. Since that time, they've used llamas to carry supplies and people across the mountainous landscape. Llamas can carry loads of 50 to 75 pounds (22.7 to 34 kg) for up to 20 miles (32.2 km) in a day.

Llamas were very important to the Inca **civilization**. The Incas didn't have cows, pigs, or sheep. They used llamas as a source of food, fuel, and clothing.

PULL BACK THE WOOL

Llamas are some of the world's oldest domesticated animals.

If a llama feels that its load is too heavy, it may not move. Llamas have been known to spit or kick at their owners until a pack is made lighter.

USEFUL ANIMALS

Today, people continue to use llamas in many ways. Llamas are easy to handle and get along well with people. Llamas can be trained to do simple jobs. Llama waste can be burned as fuel. Their **hides** can be used to make leather. Llamas are also kept for their meat.

Perhaps most importantly, llamas are kept for their wool. Llama fiber is strong. Their wool makes warm, long-lasting cloth. It can also be used to make rugs and rope.

Most llama herds are kept by people living in Bolivia, Peru, Ecuador, Chile, and Argentina.

SHEARING

A llama's coat has two layers—a **coarse** outer layer and a soft underlayer. The outer layer is made of tough hairs called guard hairs. The undercoat is made of short, soft hairs. To collect the fiber, llama owners must shear, or cut off, this coat every two years or so.

The shearing process requires teamwork. Two people hold the llama steady while one person removes its hair. Shearing doesn't hurt llamas. They're held down so they don't get cut.

PULL BACK THE WOOL

Today, shearing is often done using electric razors.

When looked at up close, llama undercoat fibers are wavy!

FROM FIBER TO FABRIC

A llama can produce about 6.6 pounds (3 kg) of fiber in one shearing. After the fiber is sheared, it's cleaned and sorted. The guard hairs make up about 20 percent of the total fiber. These hairs are longer than the soft hairs and are less **valuable**. Separating the coarse guard hairs from the soft hairs is called dehairing.

Spinning is the process by which fiber is made into yarn. Llama fiber is spun into yarn, then made into cloth, often by **weaving** or knitting.

Llama wool isn't quite as valuable as alpaca wool.

OTHER LLAMA USES

Llamas are livestock, or farm animals. Some farmers keep llamas as guard animals. For example, a llama might be kept with a herd of sheep. Since the llama is taller, it can spot predators and warn the herd.

Some people also keep llamas as pets. In the United States, llamas are now also used as therapy animals. A therapy animal's job is to offer people comfort. Therapy llamas visit nursing homes and hospitals so that people can pet them and feel happy.

PULL BACK THE WOOL

Llamas are smart! They can tell the difference between a friendly dog and a predator.

Llamas are often kept in petting zoos. They're gentle and safe for children to pet and sometimes ride.

GLOSSARY

adaptation: A change in a type of animal that makes it better able to live in its surroundings.

civilization: Organized society with written records and laws.

coarse: Having a rough quality.

communicate: To share ideas and feelings through sounds and motions.

domesticated: Bred and raised for use by people.

fiber: A thin thread of natural or human-made material that can be used to make cloth.

hide: The skin of an animal.

image: The idea that people have about someone or something.

mammal: A warm-blooded animal that has a backbone and hair, breathes air, and feeds milk to its young.

mate: To come together to make babies.

valuable: Worth money.

weave: To make cloth by passing threads back and forth over and under each other.

FOR MORE INFORMATION

Books

Brinker, Spencer. *Baby Llamas.* Minneapolis, MN: Bearport Publishing Company, 2021.

Jameson, Karen. *A Llama Is Not an Alpaca: And Other Mistaken Animal Identities.* New York, NY: Running Press Kids, 2023.

Websites

Fun Llama Facts for Kids

www.kidsplayandcreate.com/fun-llama-facts-for-kids/

Read all about llamas and even learn some llama jokes on this website.

Llama

www.nationalgeographic.com/animals/mammals/facts/llama-1

Find out everything you need to know about llamas on the National Geographic website.

Publisher's note to educators and parents: Our editors have carefully reviewed these websites to ensure that they are suitable for students. Many websites change frequently, however, and we cannot guarantee that a site's future contents will continue to meet our high standards of quality and educational value. Be advised that students should be closely supervised whenever they access the internet.

INDEX